Ideas for Jewelry

IDEAS FOR JEWELRY

Ian Davidson

B.T. BATSFORD LIMITED · LONDON
WATSON – GUPTILL PUBLICATIONS
NEW YORK

© Ian Davidson 1973

First published 1973
ISBN 0 7134 2308 0

Library of Congress Catalog
Card Number 71–190511
ISBN (USA) 8230–2525–X

Filmset by Keyspools Limited, Golborne, Lancashire
Printed Offset Litho in Great Britain by
Cox & Wyman Ltd, Fakenham, Norfolk
for the publishers
B T Batsford Limited
4 Fitzhardinge Street, London W1H 0AH and
Watson-Guptill Publications
165 West 46 Street, New York, NY 10036

Contents

Introduction   7

Materials for making models   9

Sheet materials   10

Sheet materials
Unit designs   12

Sheet materials
Random line patterns   14

Sheet materials
Metal strips   16

Working with wire
Random line patterns   20

Application of wire to
   sheet materials   22

Designing with tube and rod   28

Designing with metal bar   30

Scoring and bending   32

Textures   35

Chains   42

Sculptural designs in metal   44

Sculptural designs in wood   46

Designing with small metal
   items and metal sections   50

Metals   55
  Copper   55
  Brass   56
  Pewter   56
  Aluminium   56
  Silver   57

Equipment and tools

Basic processes   64
  Methods of cutting   64

Preparing component parts for assembly   70
  Annealing   72
  Pickling   73
  Making links   74
  Riveting   75
  Soft soldering   76
  Hard soldering   76

Methods of assembly   78

Casting methods   79
  Casting with cuttlefish bone   79
  The Solbrig casting process   84

Finishing processes   87

Further reading   90

Suppliers UK   91

Suppliers USA   92

Index   94

Colour plates by Robert Golden

Introduction

The purpose of this book is to stimulate ideas for both the design and construction of jewelry. The contents of the first section have been planned as a course in basic jewelry design, progressing through the various stages of construction, exploiting both materials and techniques to their fullest design potentialities.

Many photographs and sketches have been included to suggest ideas and help to awaken an avid awareness of the creative possibilities inherent in both materials and techniques. Obviously these suggestions are only a starting point and individual students should be able to exploit and develop each design section much more fully.

By working through the design section of the book and referring to the technical section a student should acquire both practical skill and design ability and should then be able to continue by thinking in terms of more intricate composite jewelry, combining the various skills and ideas acquired.

Jewelry should be so designed to realize the potentials of both methods of construction and materials used, rather than by trying to force the materials into a pre-conceived idea with limited skill and equipment. It is essential to realize that different materials and techniques require a different approach to design to obtain the most satisfactory results. For this reason it is stressed that an approach to jewelry design should be based on model-making and experiments with actual materials rather than on drawn designs. It is quite wrong for a student, probably unfamiliar with certain materials, to draw designs for a piece of jewelry, as this two-dimensional approach to an essentially three-dimensional craft inhibits the best use of the inherent qualities of materials. Far better results from the design point of view will be obtained if students are allowed to make models first. Careful consideration should be given to the choice of materials for modelling as they should resemble as far as possible those that are to be used for the final piece of work. For the purpose of those teaching in primary schools, it is often sufficient to regard the models as an end in themselves, for the disciplines imposed in making a model are similar in many respects to those of actually making a piece of jewelry. A model requires the same manipulation of small components, selection and grouping of materials, careful cutting and assembly but remains within the capabilities of the younger child, whereas too early an introduction to working with metal in particular, which requires physical strength in the wrist and hands, can result in frustration and consequent lack of confidence.

Consideration has been given to the necessity of working within a limited budget and for this reason tools and equipment have been kept to the minimum. However, if maximum use is made of both tools and materials very attractive jewelry can be made quite simply. It is often better to spend a larger proportion of the monies available on a variety of materials rather than on specialized, sophisticated jewelry tools.

This book is divided into two main sections: the first section deals with suggested approaches to design, and the second section provides the technical data for the various processes mentioned. Further research into certain specialized techniques such as enamelling would be necessary and reference books for this subject will be found in the bibliography.

This book is intended mainly for use in schools and colleges of education but could also be useful study for first year students of jewelry in colleges of art.

Materials for Making Models

Paper and cardboard

Cardboard tubes

Pencil and ruler

Steel ruler

Craft knife (mat knife USA) and scissors

Adhesives: PVA or *UHU* (*Elmer's* glue USA)

Pins and thread

Softboard, an insulation board marketed under various trade names. A soft fibrous board into which pins, tacks and small nails can be pressed easily

Spaghetti and various sizes of macaroni

Balsa wood in sheet and strip form of varying sizes

Wood dowelling

Beeswax, plasticine and plaster of paris

Metallic spray paint

Sheet Materials

Many interesting designs can be made very simply by cutting sheet metal or *Perspex (Plexiglas)* of varying thicknesses into shapes:
Curved shapes can be superimposed upon straight strips.

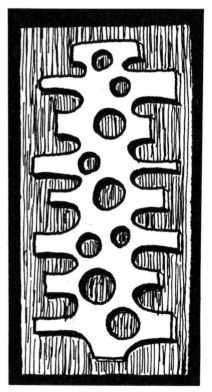

Figure 1

Intricate shapes upon simple basic shapes.

Figure 2

Identical or related shapes can be grouped together.

Contrast can be achieved with some of the shapes having a textured surface and others a plain polished surface or by using enamelling or oxidization to provide colour or tonal qualities.

Figure 3

Figure 4

Simple models using cardboard or thin sheet balsa wood should be made before working with metal or *Perspex*. Cardboard or balsa wood is very quickly cut out and glued together and several experimental designs should be tried. The models can be sprayed with metallic paint to simulate the finished product. Two or more layers of sheet metal can be joined together by lead soldering, silver soldering, riveting or adhesives. If rivets are used, then their positioning should be considered as an integral part of the design. Two or more layers of *Perspex* can be joined together with *Perspex* cement or with metal rivets.

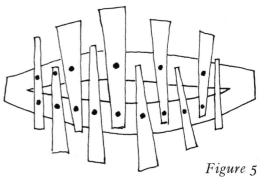

Figure 5

Sheet Materials Unit Designs

An infinite variety of ideas can be built from the combination of one or more simple basic shapes linked together in different ways. Work with a selection of shapes cut in cardboard and arrange and rearrange them in various combinations until a satisfactory design is achieved.

Units linked and repeated to form a simple bracelet suitable for either metal or *Perspex*.

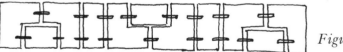

Figure 6

A linked bracelet with either superimposed shapes or cut out shapes in the larger components and with some of the smaller components textured, enamelled or oxidized. These are all ways of enriching an otherwise very simple design.

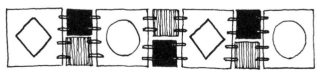

Figure 7

Linked units suitable for necklaces.

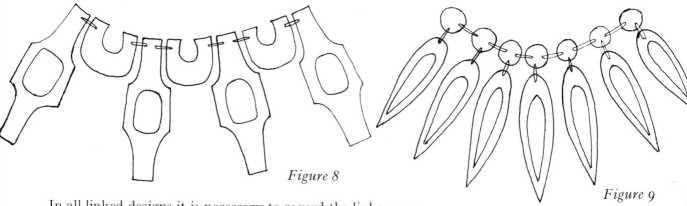

Figure 8

Figure 9

In all linked designs it is necessary to regard the links as an essential part of the design and their positioning must be carefully considered. Links may be simple wire rings or thin strips of sheet metal bent round to form a link. They can be various sizes.

Round link

Flat link

Figure 10

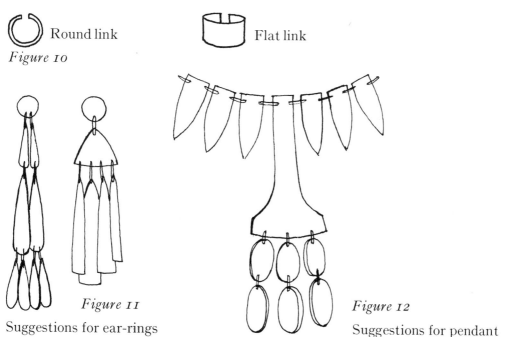

Figure 11

Suggestions for ear-rings

Figure 12

Suggestions for pendant

Sheet Materials
Random Line Patterns

Another starting point when designing with sheet materials is the use of random line patterns. Let your pencil or pen wander in a series of similar curves or straight lines or cut at random directly into a piece of paper or thin cardboard.

Studies of shells, amoeba, hydra, seaweed, cell structures and plankton would all provide reference material for designs using curved lines.

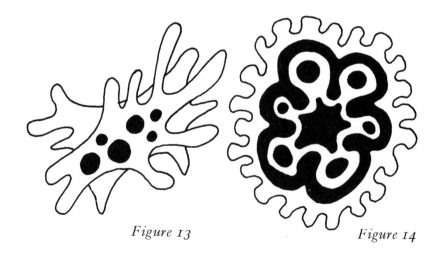

Figure 13   *Figure 14*

Studies of skylines, letter forms, hieroglyphics, graph patterns could all stimulate ideas for designs using straight lines.

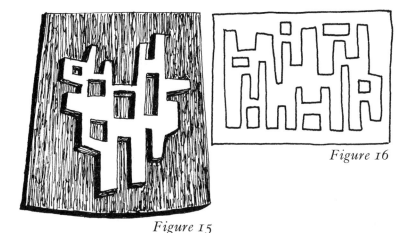

Figure 16

Figure 15

Cut out the shapes in fairly thick metal. This is especially necessary if the shapes are very intricate and delicate, for if thin sheet is used the weak points may bend or fracture. Either superimpose one shape on top of another shape, which is similar in character, or mount one shape on to a simple basic shape. Either use solder, rivets or adhesive to join the pieces together. This type of design is particularly attractive for bracelets and belts which consist of many similar component pieces.

Figure 17

Sheet Materials
Metal Strips

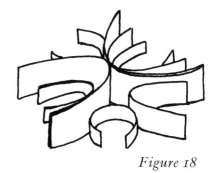

Figure 18

Do not attempt to draw designs on paper for this method. Start straight away with several strips of thin, flexible cardboard preferably cut on the guillotine or with a sharp knife and a steel ruler. The strips may vary in width from 3 mm to 10 mm ($\frac{1}{8}$ in. to 4 in.). Wider than this is unsuitable. Different widths will produce differing heights in the finished work and often the more important parts of a piece of work can be stressed by using the widest strips.

The strips of cardboard can be bent round pencils, knitting needles, dowelling or any cylindrical shape and either left in a spiral form or cut into shorter curved lengths.

For straight edge designs, mark the strips of card into lengths using a pencil and ruler and fold at each point that you have marked. Assemble all the pieces together and glue the edges to a piece of paper or card. Studies of wrought iron work, bamboo screens, flower heads and leaf shapes should all provide sources of inspiration.

Working from the cardboard model, cut thin sheet metal into strips the required widths and lengths. Roll round dowelling or steel rod for curved shapes; rectangular shapes can be obtained by pressing the strips round a steel bar. Bends in metal should always be made over a sharp steel edge, lightly tapping the strip with a hammer. Separate

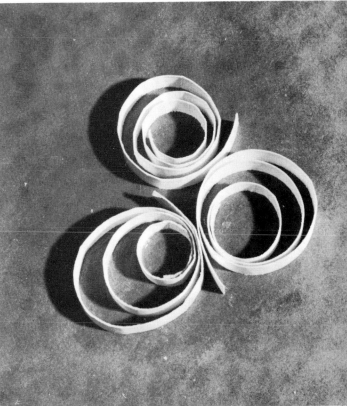

Figure 19   *Figure 20*

components can often be linked together; otherwise use solder or adhesive. It may be necessary in some designs to solder the components to a back plate of flat sheet as well, to strengthen the piece of work.

Figure 21

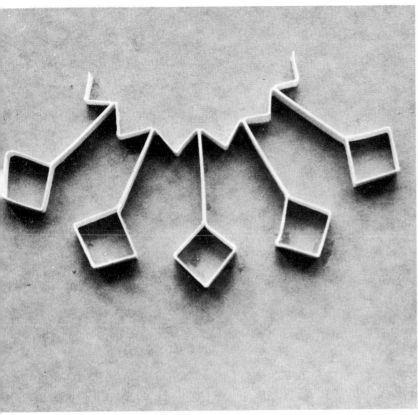

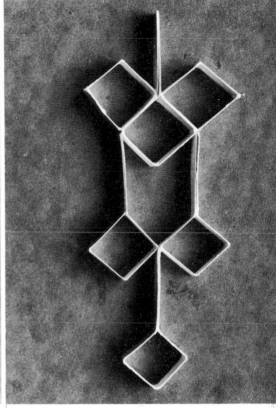

Figure 22

Figure 23

Simple band rings Metal strips of varying widths can also be used to make simple rings. First cut a strip of cardboard the required length to fit round your finger and glue together to form a ring. Next decide what sort of decoration is to be used and mark the design carefully on to the cardboard. Decoration could consist of pierced-out shapes, applied shapes or wire with some parts plain and some parts textured. A smaller ring or rings can be soldered to the basic ring.

Figure 24

Working with Wire Random Line Patterns

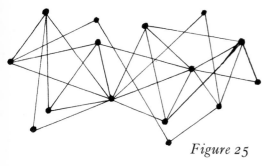

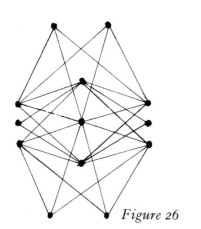

Figure 25

Figure 26

This type of design is ideal for finding ideas for wire work. Let your pen or pencil wander across the paper in a series of curves or straight lines which cross and re-cross each other at frequent intervals. Inspiration could be found by studying textural patterns such as rock strata, smoke patterns, lightning, frost patterns on windows and water. Another way of obtaining ideas is by placing a few dressmakers' pins at random into a piece of softboard and then winding thread from one pin to another (*figure 25*). More formal or geometrical designs can be achieved by placing a piece of graph paper (10 squares represent 25 mm (1 in.)) over insulation board and then placing the pins in a symmetrical pattern and winding the thread from one pin to another as previously. Many different designs can be obtained from the same arrangement of pins. Studies of snow crystals, crystalline structures, rock structures and star formations could all provide inspiration for this type of design (*figures 26 and 27*).

To reproduce this type of design using wire, hammer small nails or panel pins (carpet tacks) into a piece of wood. One nail is required for each bend in the design: bend the wire round the nails following the original design. The wires can be soldered together where they overlap to give strength to the piece of work, or they can be soldered to a backplate cut from sheet metal to serve as brooches, or pendants.

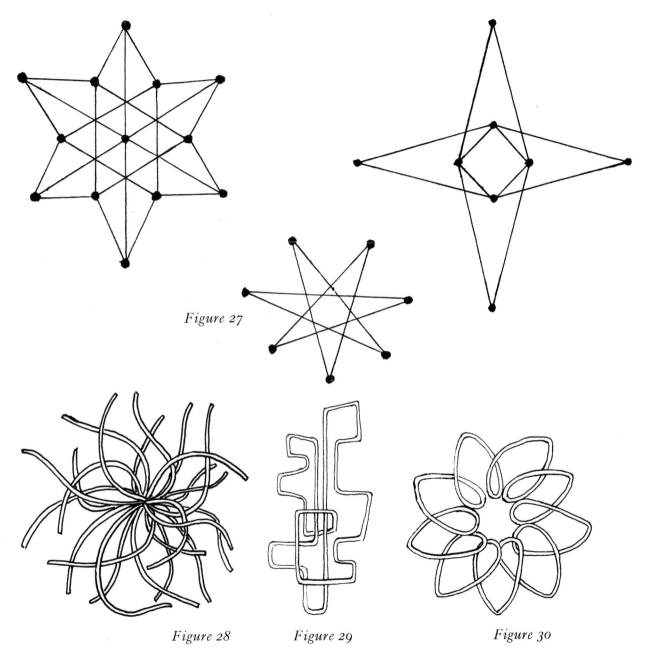

Figure 27

Figure 28   *Figure 29*   *Figure 30*

Application of Wire to Sheet Materials

Attractive pieces of jewelry can be made by simply applying straight lengths of wire to a flat metal shape. Added interest can be achieved by piercing out parts of the metal shape, adding beads or half-drilled pearls, or by making a loop on the ends of the wires and hooking them on to a thin strip so that they are free to move.

Using cardboard to simulate the metal shape, and lengths of spaghetti to simulate the wire, make models of your ideas. These models look very realistic if they are sprayed with metallic paint. Beads or pearls can be glued on after spraying.

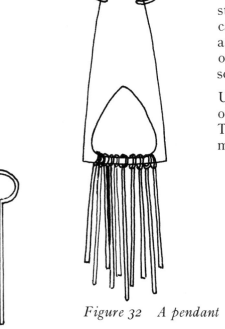

Figure 32   A pendant

Figure 31   Loop on the end of wire

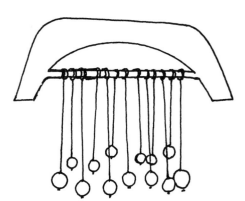

Figure 33   A brooch

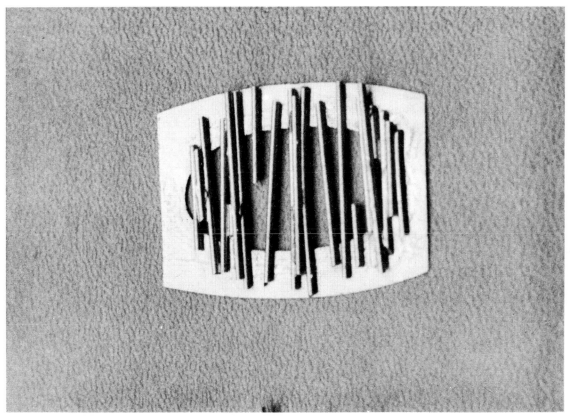

Models of ideas for rings and bangles can be made by either bending strips of cardboard into rings or by sawing off slices from cardboard tubes.

Figure 34

Figure 35

Figure 36

It is possible to obtain cardboard tubes in a variety of sizes. For circular radial designs ideas could be found from studying flower heads, dandelion clocks, wheels, or by slicing through tomatoes, peppers, oranges, etc.

Short lengths of wire can be grouped together in clusters, stood up on end and mounted on a metal plate.

Figure 37

Figure 38

Figure 39

25

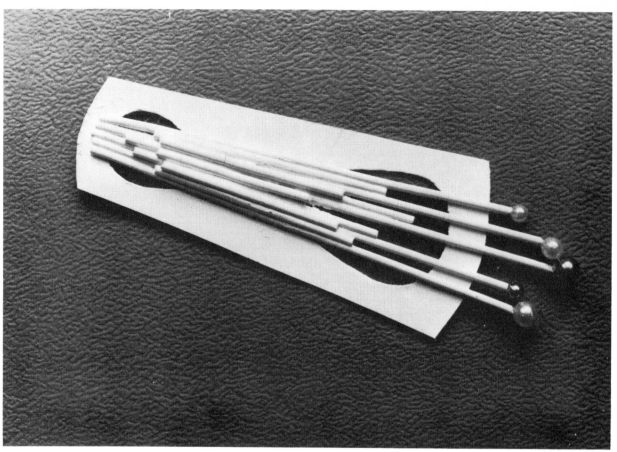

Figure 40

Studies of different shaped string instruments are particularly suitable as most of them are a very attractive shape and they have other shapes cut out with the strings or wires going over them.

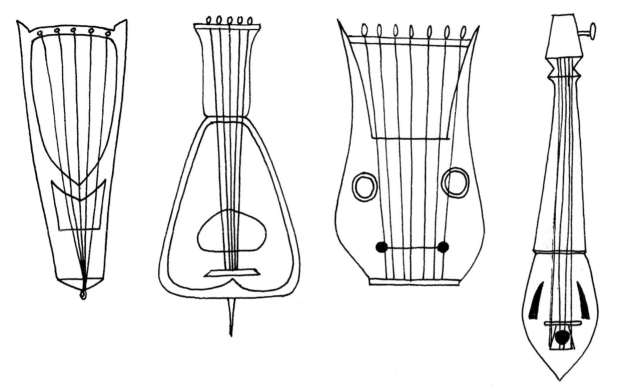

Figure 41

Designing with Tube and Rod

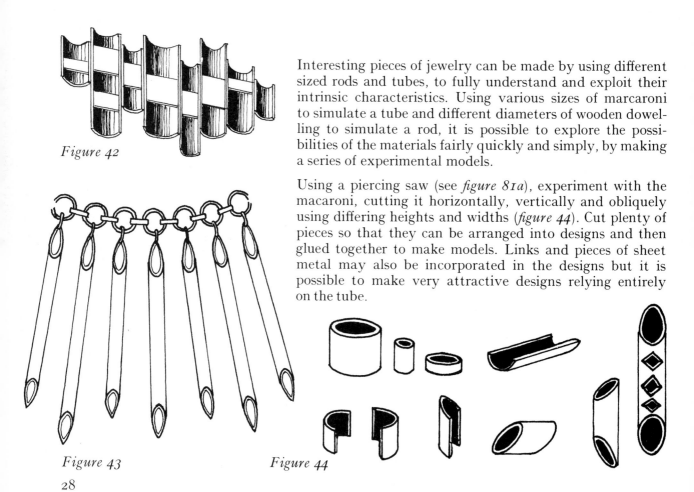

Figure 42

Interesting pieces of jewelry can be made by using different sized rods and tubes, to fully understand and exploit their intrinsic characteristics. Using various sizes of marcaroni to simulate a tube and different diameters of wooden dowelling to simulate a rod, it is possible to explore the possibilities of the materials fairly quickly and simply, by making a series of experimental models.

Using a piercing saw (see *figure 81a*), experiment with the macaroni, cutting it horizontally, vertically and obliquely using differing heights and widths (*figure 44*). Cut plenty of pieces so that they can be arranged into designs and then glued together to make models. Links and pieces of sheet metal may also be incorporated in the designs but it is possible to make very attractive designs relying entirely on the tube.

Figure 43

Figure 44

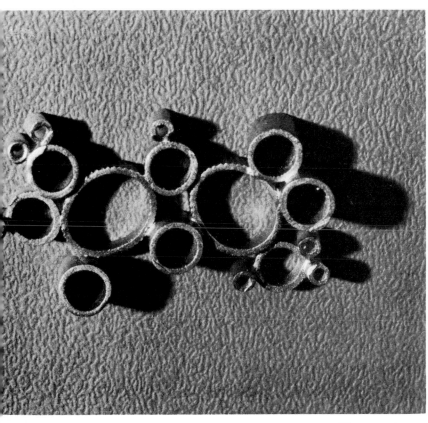

Figure 45

Figure 46

Studies of lichen, fungi, pebbles, etc could provide ideas for random arrangements of horizontally cut sections of tube. Ideas for more formal arrangements could come from studying chimney-pots, smoke-stacks, drain-pipes and scaffolding.

Figure 47

29

Designing with Metal Bar

Metal can be obtained in different sizes and sections, square or rectangular, in strip form called metal bar. The variety of sizes provides sufficiently interesting material to make exciting designs without the use of any other forms of metal, although of course other forms of metal, *Perspex*, or wood can be used in conjunction with the metal bar. Use strips of balsa wood of different sizes and sections to simulate the metal bar. Make experimental models by cutting a variety of different lengths of balsa wood, sticking them together with glue and spraying the finished model with metallic spray paint. It is technically much simpler to keep metal bar in straight lengths, and interesting effects can be achieved by cutting and filing (*figures 48, 49 and 50*). It can, however, be bent as long as the degree of bend required is fairly shallow.

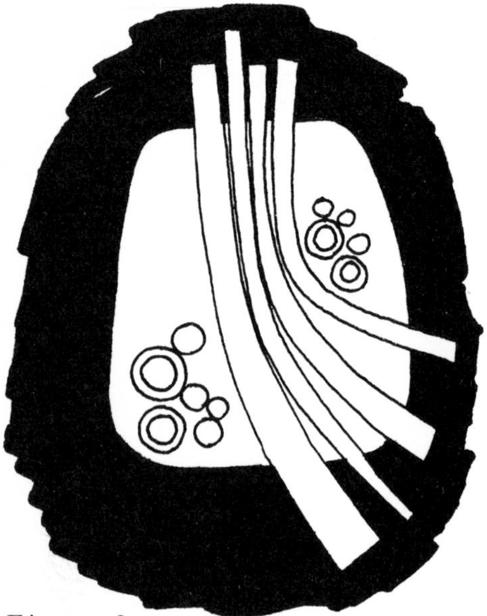

Figure 48

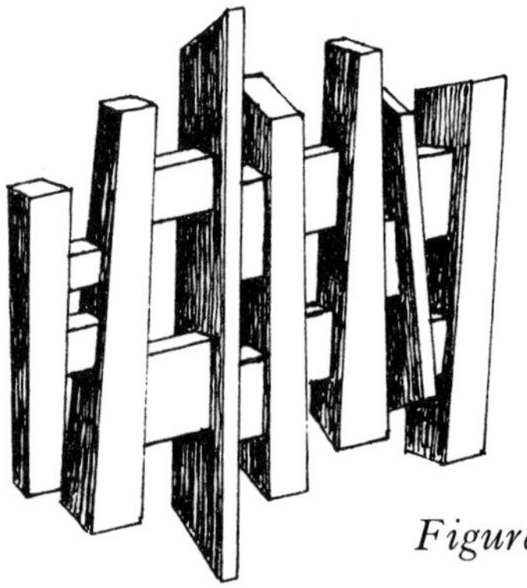

Figure 49

Figure 50

Figure 51

Ideas for working with this type of material can be found from studying brick and stone walls, rock strata, wood in a lumber yard or books in a bookcase.

As metal bar is much heavier than wire or sheet, this must be considered carefully, particularly when designing earrings and brooches.

Scoring and Bending

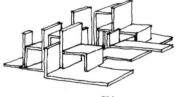

Figure 52

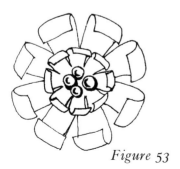

Figure 53

Designs of a more three-dimensional nature can be made by simply cutting out shapes in cardboard and scoring and bending them, either in geometrical designs (*figures 52 and 54*) or in more natural forms (*figure 53*). It must, however, be remembered that although cardboard can be scored and folded into very intricate forms, the possibilities with metal are more limited. It is necessary, therefore, to restrict the number of bends in each component part to not more than two on fairly large pieces and only one on smaller pieces, otherwise it would be too difficult to retain the preciseness of the technique without considerable skill and an unlimited collection of tools. Both the cardboard models and the finished pieces of jewelry require the discipline of accurate cutting, scoring and fitting together to achieve successful results.

Both thick and very thin metal can be used for this type of design. Attractive rings can be made using thick metal by bending and hammering round a triblet (mandrel) or steel rod or bar.

Thinner metal can be bent over a steel edge mainly by finger pressure alone but it may be necessary to lightly hammer the bend to produce a crisp edge.

Figure 54

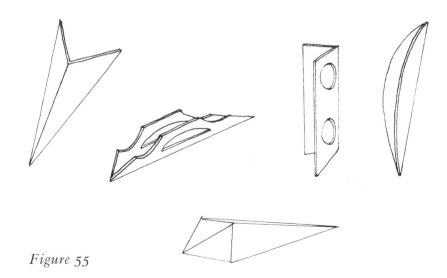

Figure 55

Figure 56

33

Figure 57

This type of design is particularly suitable for pendant earrings and necklaces (*figure 57* gives suggestions for components which could be used either singly or several of the same shape soldered together), and for simple rings, but with increasing skill and imagination it can also be used to produce very successful brooches, pendants and bracelets.

Textures

The smooth surface of metal can be textured in many ways to provide a contrast, added interest and greater sparkle to a piece of jewelry. Textures can be simply achieved by using various hammers or by using a hammer and various nails. The former produces patterns that are indented into the metal and this type of texturing therefore requires fairly thick pieces of metal; and the latter produces raised patterns on one side and indented patterns on the other and requires thinner pieces of metal.

Metal textured by hammering requires a hard metal surface as a support, a piece of smooth plate steel, an anvil or the sole-plate of an old iron can be used for this. The head of the hammer must be smooth and polished as any small cuts or scratches in the hammer head will be transferred blow by blow to the metal. It is possible to shape the head of the hammer on a grinding machine to a particularly desired shape.

For areas of texture it is advisable to first anneal the metal to make it more malleable. It is better to texture an area larger than that required as the edges become distorted with the hammering. The surplus metal can be sawn off, leaving an even crisp edge to the shape.

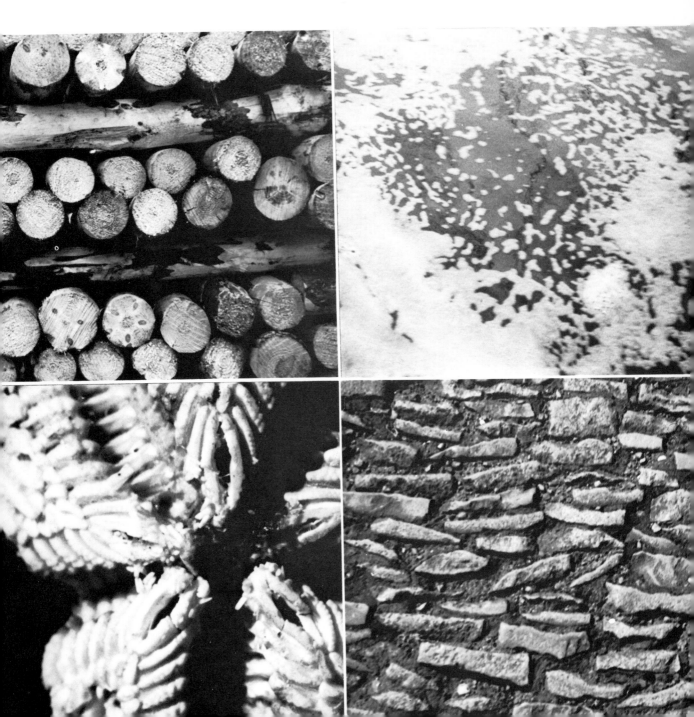

Figure 62 shows textures made with a mason's hammer shaped on a grinding machine.

◄ *Figures 58–61   Textures photographed from the environment*
Top left   Stacked logs
Top right   Foam on water
Bottom left   Detailed close-up of star fish
Bottom right   Irregular stone wall

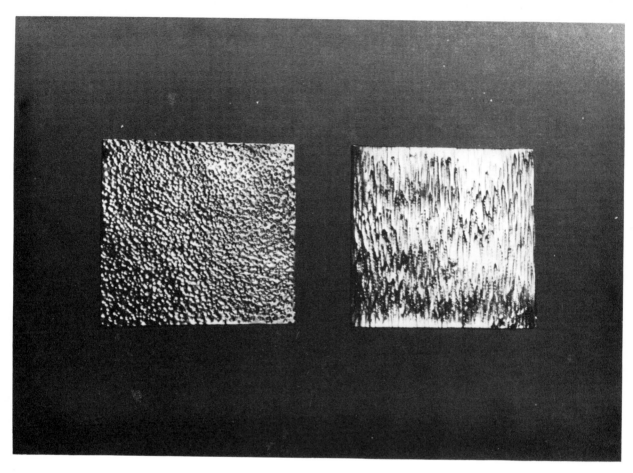

Figure 63 shows texture made with a ball pein hammer, riveting hammer or the ball end of a repoussé hammer and using a sharp neck hammer, cross pein or Warrington hammer.

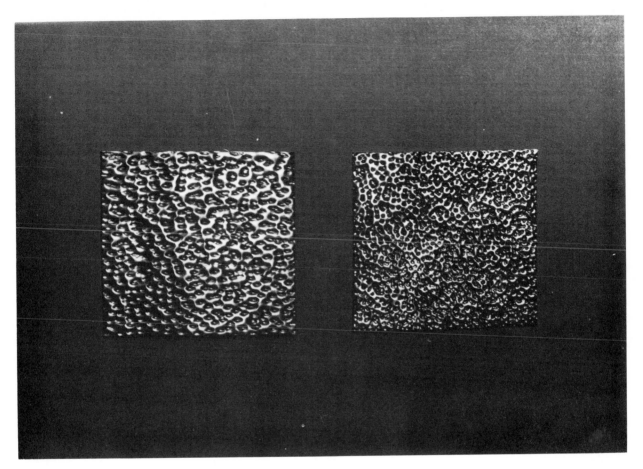

Figure 64 shows textures obtained by hammering the point
and the edge of the head of a nail into thin metal on a lead
block.

Figure 65 shows the method of using the point of a nail to form a texture.

Figure 66 shows the method of using the edge of a nail head
to form a texture.

Chains

It is possible to buy lengths of chain or to utilize pieces cut from old jewelry, but it is infinitely more satisfying to make your own. The design of the chain from which to hang pendants or to complete a necklet can be considered at the same time as the design of the actual pendant or necklet, and they can then complement each other and form an attractive unit with the colour of the metal the same for each part.

An infinite variety of chains, both in size and design, can be made very simply from a combination of different basic shapes and various shaped links. Component parts may be made of pieces cut from sheet metal or *Perspex*, wire forms or sections cut from tubes or a combination of any of these (*figure 67*). Chain does not have to be made entirely of metal components. Interesting designs can be achieved by making extended links and threading glass or wooden beads on to these.

Chain can be used as a piece of jewelry in itself, either singly for bracelets or on a very much larger scale for belts, or several chains either of similar or differing designs can be worn collectively.

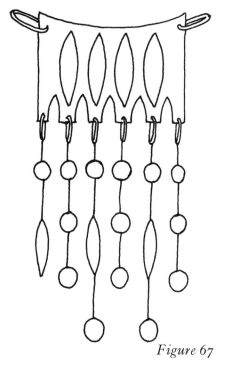

Figure 67

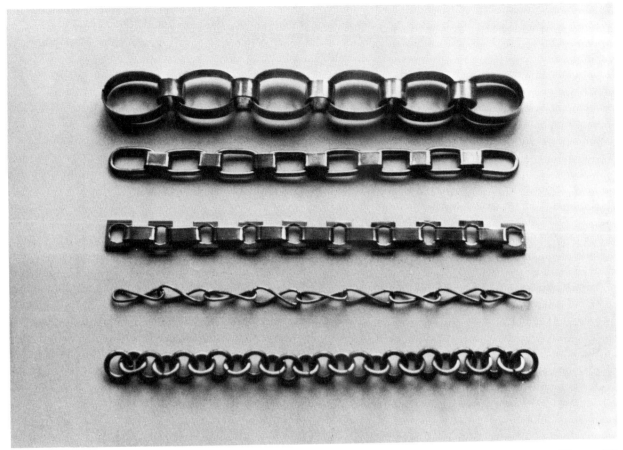

Figure 68

A study of Victorian jewelry would provide many examples of the design and use of chain. Ideas might also be found by exploring a junk-yard or shipyard for different approaches to the problem of linking component parts together into a strong integrated whole.

Sculptural Designs in Metal

Jewelry of a more sculptural nature requires different techniques, both in the design and manufacture, from those methods previously mentioned. This type of jewelry is generally much heavier in weight but less restricted in design because of the way that it is made by pouring molten metal into a mould.

A simple casting technique such as gravity pouring using pewter as the metal and cuttlefish bone for the mould will produce quite detailed sculptural or relief designs. Steam pressure casting will produce similar designs but it is also possible to produce much finer, more intricate designs such as filigree work with this method.

Both methods are more suitable for individual, 'one off', designs such as pendants and brooches rather than for component parts of a necklace or bracelet. It is possible to incorporate semi-precious or synthetic stones into this type of design by carefully considering the positions of the claws for holding the stones, and including them in the design when making the mould. It is preferable to make models in wax before attempting to make a mould and it must be remembered that to reproduce the wax model in metal, the design must be visualized in reverse. It is possible to create attractive designs in relief by simply pressing various implements directly into the cuttlefish bone without making any

Figure 69

previous model or design. Experience in controlling this approach to designing for this technique can only be achieved by practice.

Beeswax is the most suitable type of wax to use for making models. It is easy to carve into various planes or shapes with a knife, to texture with various small implements such as nails, files etc and if it is cut into fairly thin slices holes can be melted in the wax with hot wire. A hot wire can also be used to fuse two or more pieces of wax together. Thin slices of wax can also be manipulated in the hands if the wax is first warmed slightly to make it more plastic.

Ideas for sculptural designs could be evolved by studying natural forms such as rock formations, uncut crystalline structures, shells, seed-pods, etc.

Sculptural Designs in Wood

Wood is an ideal material for sculptural designs: it is easy to carve, file and polish it into beautiful smooth forms. Wood varies considerably in hardness, colour and grain and these variations should be considered when choosing a piece of wood for a certain type of design.

Several different approaches can be made to designing wooden jewelry if full use is made of the natural qualities of the wood itself and the natural patterns derived from working with certain tools. The best designs are often the simplest, using only one basic tool to provide a textural pattern to the surface of the wood or choosing a piece of wood with maybe a knot in it or with an interesting tonal or colour change, and cutting and polishing it into a simple abstract shape. Imaginative use of tools such as files, drills, counter-sink drills and gouges can all be used as a way of approaching design by using the tool as an end in itself rather than as a means to an end (*figure 70* opposite. See also colour plate facing page 73).

Plasticine or plaster models can be made of simple sculptural forms before starting to work with wood itself, but it would probably be better to choose a piece of wood first and then consider how the design could enhance its characteristics. Experiments should be made with various tools to discover the design potential of the tools themselves. Variety of

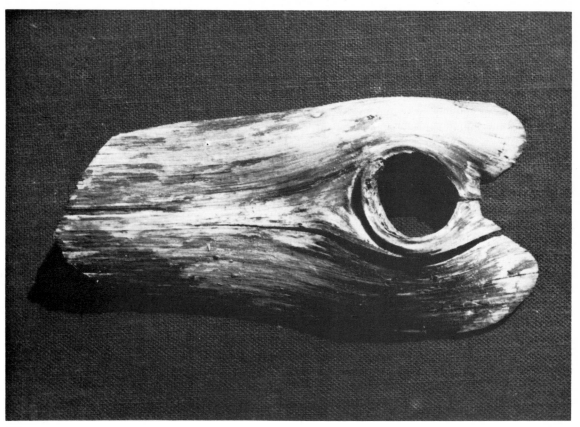

Figure 71

design can be achieved by using several different sizes of one tool rather than by trying to use too many tools on one small piece of wood. Softer woods such as pine can also have a design burnt into them by heating a metal tool or a specially shaped piece of metal red-hot, and pressing it into the wood.

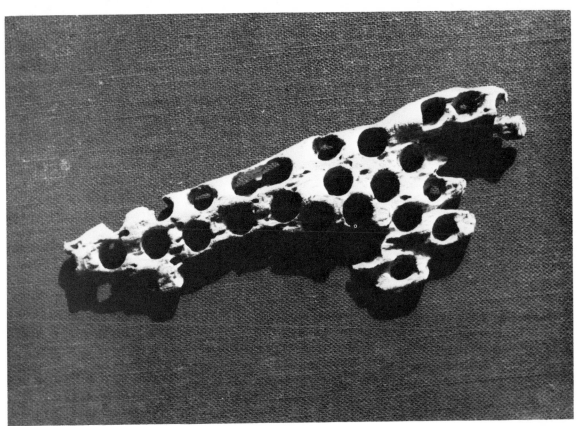

Figure 72

Designing with Small Metal Items and Metal Sections

Various small manufactured items such as rivets, eyelets, washers, nuts, drawing pins (thumbtacks), upholstery tacks, (*figure 74*) can be obtained from most hardware stores or 'do-it-yourself' shops. It is important to make sure that the items are either brass or copper and not just plated, as plated items will not withstand high temperatures and would therefore be unsuitable for soldering. It is often possible to obtain items in more than one size, which is a great advantage when designing.

Other small interesting metal shapes can be obtained by purchasing lengths of various sections and sawing them into a collection of shapes of varying depth. The most interesting metal sections are only available in brass. It is possible to obtain U or channel sections, L or angle sections, hexagonal rods and square tubes from sheet metal suppliers. I or T-sections can be obtained by collecting pieces of old brass curtain rail; the brass pulleys could also be used either as they are or in separate pieces.

Designs should be derived from arranging and re-arranging the various items listed, either working with one item alone and using various sizes, or by combining two or three different items together. The most successful designs are

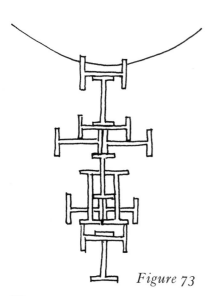

Figure 73

usually those which only use one or two items. The interest is derived from the relationship of one component to another and the various shapes that come between them.

It is possible to incorporate either wood or *Perspex* as well as metal as a base for these small items, for instance holes could be drilled into either wood or *Perspex* and various sized rivets or drawing pins could be fixed into these holes with adhesive.

Figure 77

53

Figure 78

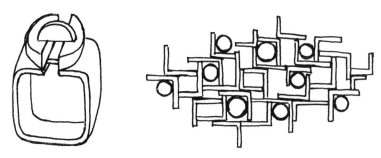

Figure 79

Figure 80

54

Metals

The metals required are in two categories: those for general purpose work and those for casting. Brass and copper are the most suitable base metals for general purpose work, and pewter and aluminium are the most suitable base metals for casting. Of the precious metals, silver is the cheapest and an ideal metal for both general purpose work and casting.

Copper Copper can be bought in sheet form in various thicknesses (gauges) known as Imperial Standard Wire Gauge (ISWG) in the UK and Brown and Sharp (USA). Sheets are normally 120 cm × 60 cm (4 ft × 2 ft) but smaller specified amounts can be ordered. A suitable selection of gauges would be 14, 18, 22 and 24, the smaller number denoting the greater thickness.

Copper is also obtainable in tubular form in various diameters. The measurement for copper tubing is the inside diameter and suitable sizes would be from 6 mm to 25 mm ($\frac{1}{4}$ in. to 1 in.) graduating in measures of 3 mm (eighths of an inch). Copper bought as tubing, wire, bar, strip or rod can all be ordered by the centimetre foot).

Copper strip is obtainable from 3 mm × 1·5 mm ($\frac{1}{8}$ in. × $\frac{1}{16}$ in.) to 50 mm × 3 mm (2 in. × $\frac{1}{8}$ in.). Rectangular bar is available from 6 mm × 3 mm ($\frac{1}{4}$ in. × $\frac{1}{8}$ in.) to 12 mm × 6 mm ($\frac{1}{2}$ in. × $\frac{1}{4}$ in.) graduating in millimetres (sixteenths of an inch).

Copper is also available in wire form, either as round wire, half-round wire or square wire in various gauges. Round wire over 3 mm ($\frac{1}{8}$ in.) in diameter is known as rod and can be obtained up to 12 mm ($\frac{1}{2}$ in.) diameter. The melting point of copper is 1083°C.

Brass   Brass is available in the same sizes and varieties as listed for copper and is also available in the following forms: Extra thin gauges are available in sheet form known as brass shim. This is available in coils from 6 mm ($\frac{1}{4}$ in.) wide and suitable gauges would be 0·132 mm (0·005 in.), 0·254 mm (0·010 in.), and 0·376 mm (0·015 in.). Brass shim is extremely flexible and easy to manipulate, very suitable for coiling and bending. The measurement for brass tubing is the outside diameter and brass tubing is also available in square section as well as round.

Hexagonal wire is available in brass in sizes from 3 mm to 12 mm ($\frac{1}{8}$ in. to $\frac{1}{2}$ in.) and angle section and channel or U-section can also be obtained. The melting point of brass is 940°C.

Pewter   Pewter is an ideal metal for casting when using simple casting techniques, as it has such a low melting point. It is, however, a very heavy metal and this should be taken into consideration when making the mould.

Pewter is only available in sheet form from sheet metal suppliers, although it might be possible to collect old, damaged pewter articles from junkyards or junk shops. These could then be cut into small pieces and melted down in a plumber's ladle and then used for casting.

The melting point of pewter is 295°C.

Aluminium   Aluminium is a suitable metal for casting. It provides strong, smooth and very much lighter castings than pewter but as its melting point is higher than pewter, it requires considerably more heat to melt it.

Aluminium is available in sheet and ingot form; casting aluminium should be specified when ordering.

The melting point of aluminium is 660°C.

Silver This is an ideal metal for all types of jewelry techniques. It is a very malleable and ductile metal which makes it easy to work with, and it is possible to polish it to a very high finish. It is, of course, more expensive than any of the other metals mentioned but it can be purchased in very small quantities, in inches rather than in feet, and it is available in a wide range of forms and sizes.

Standard silver is the most commonly used, because fine silver, which is a pure metal, is rather too soft for general work. Standard silver is an alloy of 925 parts silver and 75 parts copper.

The melting point of standard silver is 893°C.

Equipment and Tools

This list is made up of the basic requirements for the techniques mentioned in the book. If the techniques were limited it would be possible to shorten the list, particularly for those setting up for the first time and on a very small budget. Obviously this list of tools is by no means complete; as greater skill is acquired and more ambitious work is attempted, then more specialized tools will need to be added to the list.

Basic essential requirements

Bench peg
Work-bench
Engineer's vice
Gas ring
Electric soldering iron
Electric polishing motor or, alternatively, an electric power drill with tapered spindle

Tools
Piercing saw frame and assorted saw blades (*figure 81a*)

Junior eclipse saw (*figure 81b*)
Coping saw (*figure 81c*)
Tenon saw
Hand drill and assorted twist drills and countersink drills
Centre punch
Straight shears—small and large
Tweezers
Pliers: round nose, snipe nose, flat nose and ring pliers (*figure 82*)

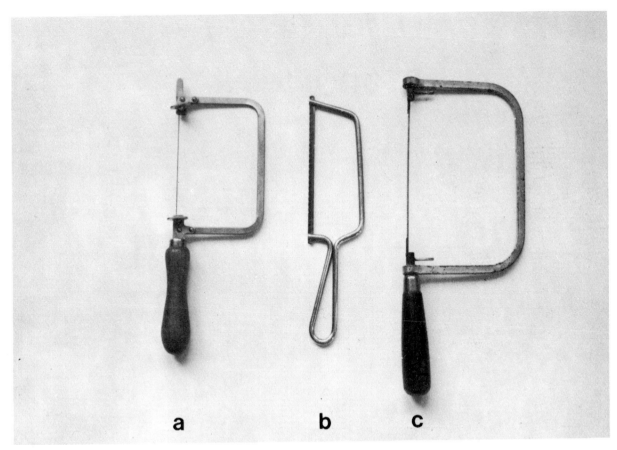

Figure 81
a   Piercing saw
b   Junior eclipse saw
c   Coping saw

Steel rule (*figure 83a*)
Scriber (*figure 83b*)
Spring dividers (*figure 83e*)
Hammers: Engineer's ball
    pein hammer, ball head
    hammer, creasing ham-
    mer, planishing hammer
    and chasing hammer
    (*figure 84 a–e*)

Hide mallet
Hand vice, pin vice and pin
    chuck
Lead or hardwood block
    and steel surface plate, or
    the sole plate of an old
    iron
Files: 203 mm (8 in.) hand
    files both rough cut and

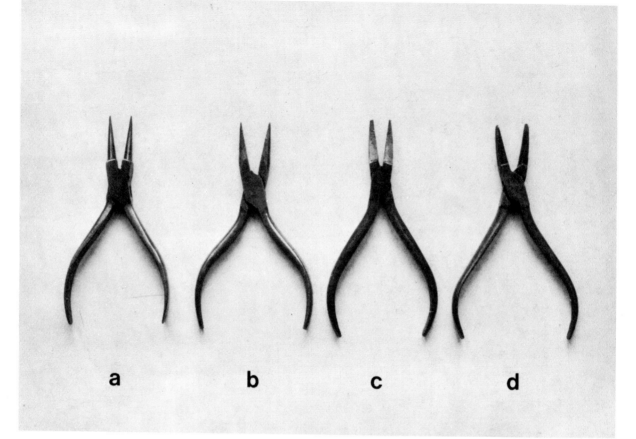

Figure 82
a   Round nose
b   Snipe nose
c   Flat nose
d   Ring pliers

smooth cut in round,
half-round, square and
three-square and file
handles
Assorted needle files
Ring triblet (mandrel)
Ring sizes
Pyrex glass dish
French blowpipe (*Mallotte*)

Borax tray and cone
Paint brush
Plumber's ladle

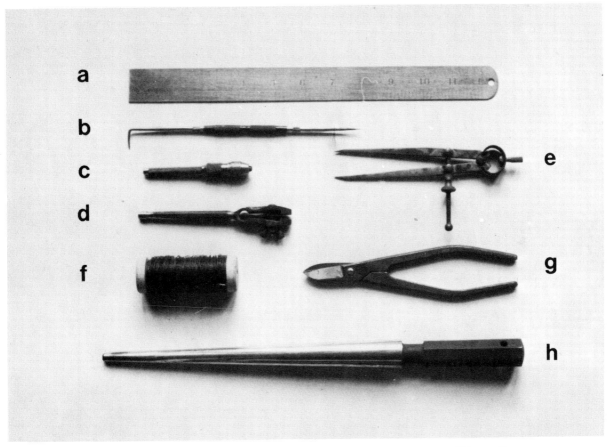

Figure 83
a   *Steel rule*
b   *Scriber*
c   *Pin chuck*
d   *Pin vice*
e   *Spring dividers*
f   *Reel of binding wire*
g   *Small jeweler's shears*
h   *Ring triblet*

Materials and sundries
Safety pickle (*Sparex*)
Silver solder and tinsman's
    solder
Baker's fluid
Asbestos blocks and sheet
Iron binding wire
Emery paper and garnet
    paper

Tripoli and rouge composi-
    tion
Silver polish and furniture
    polish
Polishing lathe mops and
    brushes and ring felts
Cuttlefish bone
Asbestos blocks
Perspex (Plexiglas) cement

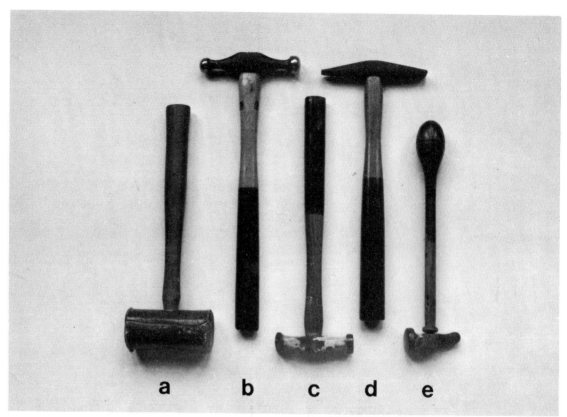

Figure 84
a Hide mallet
b Ball pein hammer
c Planishing hammer
d Creasing hammer
e Chasing hammer

and *Araldite* epoxy
Fire-clay bricks
Assorted nails
Investment materials
Plaster of paris
Beads
Collection of small manu-
    factured items
Findings

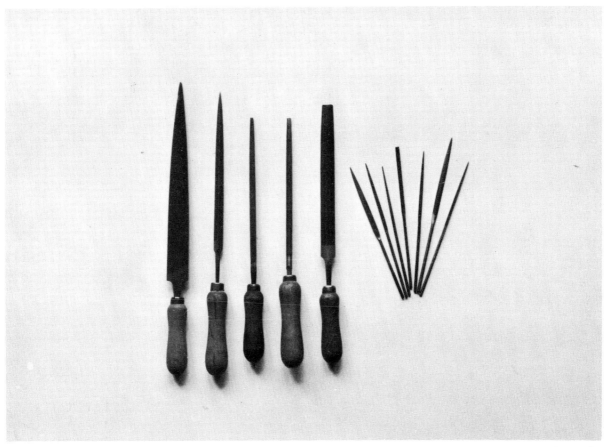

Figure 85

Basic Processes

Methods of Cutting

The piercing saw is one of the most important tools used by a jeweler. It is possible, with practice and experience, to cut very intricate shapes in sheet metal with great accuracy. Mastery of this process will eliminate unnecessary time spent filing. It is therefore important that the function of the saw frame and blade is fully understood.

There are various types and sizes of saw frames. For general jewelry purposes, the most useful size is a 76 mm (3 in.). This measurement is the distance between the blade and the frame. Larger sized frames are not recommended for beginners as they increase the risk of blade breakage.

Piercing saw blades can be obtained in various grades which are specified by numbers. No. 2 is a coarse blade and no. 8/0 is very fine. A no. 2 blade is suitable for sawing thick sheet metal such as 14 and 16 ISWG (Brown and Sharp) and no. 8/0 for brass shim. The main principle for selecting the right size of blade is that at least two teeth on the saw blade should cover the edge of the metal. The selection of the wrong size will cause unnecessary blade breakage. To place a blade in the frame: first see that the teeth of the blade are

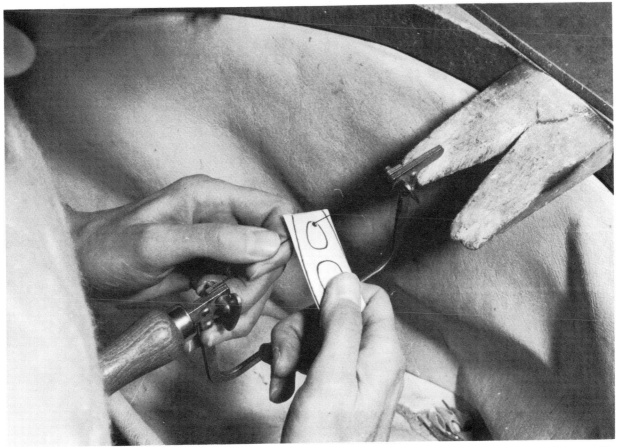

Figure 86

pointing downwards towards the handle, then clamp the
blade into the frame at the opposite end from the handle.
This should be done with hand pressure only. If pliers are
used to tighten the thumb screws they will overhaul the
thread. To clamp the other end of the blade in the frame,
place the handle of the frame against the body and the other
end of the frame against the bench, and apply slight pressure
whilst clamping the blade at the handle end. This pressure is
necessary as the blade should be in a state of tension in the
frame, otherwise breakage will occur.

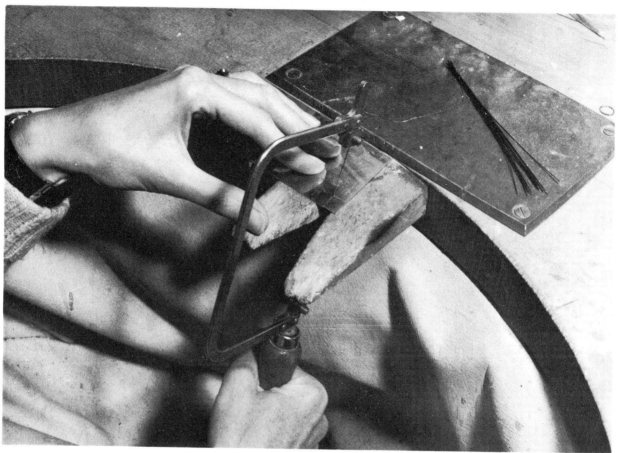

Figure 87

It is suggested that the shape or design to be sawn out is first drawn on a piece of paper which can then be glued to the metal and will protect its surface while the saw piercing is carried out. Before commencing sawing out, prepare the bench peg for this process by cutting out a V-shaped notch from the front edge (*figure 87*). The sheet metal to be cut should rest on the bench peg and the saw frame should be held in a vertical position (*figure 88*). The saw blade should move upwards and downwards with slightly more pressure applied to the downward movement.

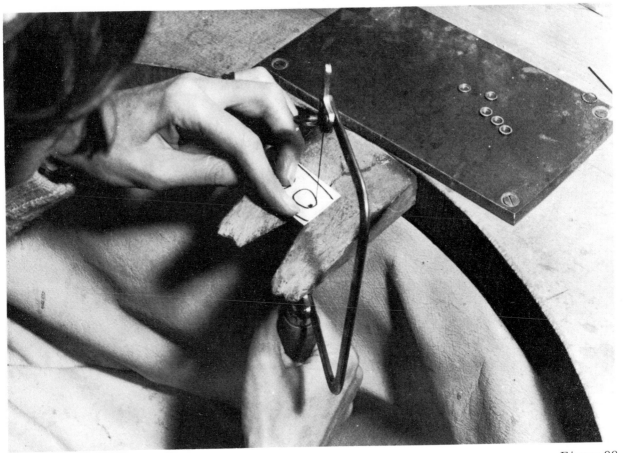

Figure 88

Where totally enclosed parts have to be sawn out, it is
necessary to drill a hole first and then to thread the saw
blade through and re-clamp the blade into the frame.

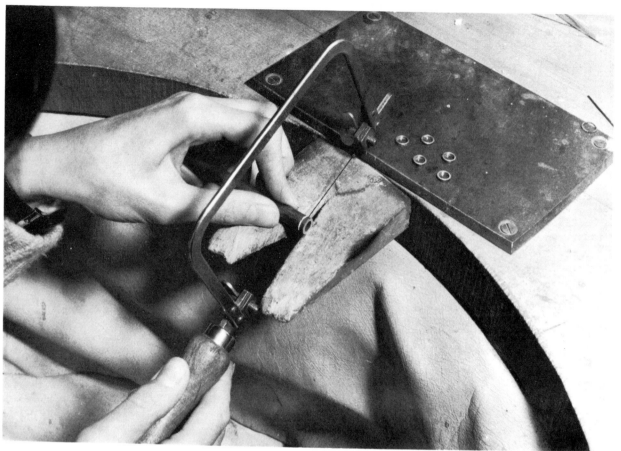

Figure 89

The saw frame and blade can also be used for cutting wire and thin wall tube. The blade should be in a more horizontal position for sawing these forms of metal.

Figure 90

Other forms of metal and other materials require different cutting tools. Thin sheet metal such as brass shim can be easily cut with jeweler's shears and thicker gauges can be cut with larger sized shears held in a vice (*figure 90*). A Junior Eclipse saw should be used to cut metal rod and other heavy sections. *Perspex* and wood should be cut with a coping saw.

Preparing Component Parts for Assembly

Before assembling component parts it is necessary to smooth the cut or sawn edges by filing and for certain assembly methods to buff the edges as well. A selection of files of various shapes and sizes are required. A flat or hand file is required for straight edges, concave curves require a half-round file and sharp corners may require either a square or three-square file. Best results will be obtained if care is taken in the selection of the right type of file for the purpose. It is preferable to use as large a file as possible, as this is both quicker and leaves a smoother finish. Very intricate shapes necessitate the use of a selection of different shaped needle files, however.

To assist in holding small components, there are several useful tools available such as a hand vice, pin vice and flat nosed pliers. These are recommended if available as they save considerable wear and tear on fingernails! It is possible to file several identical shapes at the same time by using a hand vice with small pieces of cardboard for protective clamps. This accelerates the process and provides uniformity of shape.

It is important to keep files clean and free from clogging by brushing them with a wire brush or file card. As softer metals such as pewter and wood and *Perspex* tend to clog files more quickly than harder metals, it is preferable to have a separate set of files for each material.

Components that are to be assembled by linking together

Figure 91

should be buffed as well as filed, using emery paper or cloth
for metal and garnet paper for wood or *Perspex*. This further
process should remove all scratch and file marks at this stage
as it is often very difficult to get access to certain edges when
linked together. These buffing materials can be wrapped
round files or shaped pieces of wood which are selected for
their similarity to the shape to be buffed.

Always drill against a wooden support as this protects the
tip of the drill from damage (*figure 91*). Select a drill with a
slightly larger diameter than that of the wire links to be

Figure 92

used. For flat links it is necessary to drill two holes slightly wider apart than the link itself and then saw pierce between the two holes to form a slot.

Annealing It is preferable to soften wire or strip before bending by annealing. This process makes the metal more pliable and malleable and less liable to stress. To anneal metal heat with a blow-torch until the metal is a dull red colour. Overheating will result in the metal melting. Quench the hot metal in cold water immediately after annealing and then place in the heated 'safety pickle'.

Figure 93

Pickling This is always necessary after annealing in order to remove oxides formed on the surface of the metal during annealing. A recommended method of pickling is to dissolve 'safety pickle' (*Sparex*) in water in the ratio of 142 grams (5 oz) to 0·6 litres (1 pint). This can be placed in a heat-proof glass dish and heated to just under boiling point on a tripod over a gas ring. 'Safety pickle' is recommended for use in schools rather than sulphuric acid which is an alternative pickle but which could prove dangerous.

Figure 94

Making links Links can be formed by bending wire or strip round any available metal rod or drill shank for round links (*figure 93*), flat links can be bent round metal bar, chisels or jaws of flat nosed pliers (*figure 94*). After bending remove the coiled wire and saw or cut the coil into separate rings. It is necessary to make flat links one at a time but several round wire links can be made at the same. By experimenting with nails (which have their heads removed) hammered into a block of wood, it is possible to make more complicated shapes and twisted links.

RIVETING Riveting is one of the oldest and simplest methods of joining sheet metal together and metal to other materials such as leather. Rivets are both functional and decorative, therefore their positioning should be considered as an integral part of the design.

Rivets can be used for metal and *Perspex*, provided that in the case of *Perspex* the rivets are glued into the drilled holes rather than hammered in, as in the case of metal. Hammering would shatter *Perspex*.

Rivets can be bought or made from wire and should be carefully selected for appearance and size. A rivet should have a diameter of at least twice the thickness of the metal being riveted. Rivets must be in an annealed state to allow the metal to spread or form a head when hammered. Bought ones are usually already annealed, rivets made from wire must be annealed. The length of the rivet is very important, it should be the thickness of the metal plus one and a half times the rivet diameter when forming cup heads and plus half the rivet diameter for countersunk heads. The length of rivets for *Perspex* should be the exact thickness of the *Perspex*. There are various shaped heads for rivets, most bought rivets are cup head and these and countersunk heads would be the simplest to use.

Countersunk rivets Drilled holes must be slightly countersunk at either side to accept the rivet head. Either use a slightly larger drill or use a countersink drill for this purpose. Wire rivets should protrude by half the rivet diameter from either side. To form countersunk rivets, place the metal to be riveted on a steel plate and hammer the rivet with the ball end of a chasing hammer to spread the rivet, repeat for the opposite side until the rivet is flush with the metal.

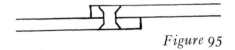

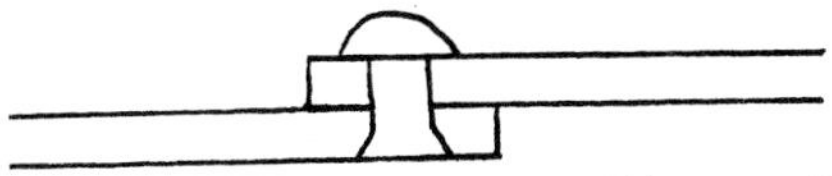

Figure 95

Cup head rivets For this method it is necessary to protect the existing cup head by drilling a hole of corresponding size to the cup head in a piece of hard wood or metal bar. Countersink one side of the drilled hole which will become the back of the work and then thread the rivet through with the cup head resting in the protective hole and hammer the rivet

Figure 96

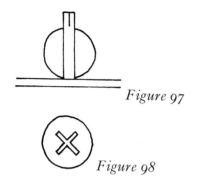

Figure 97

Figure 98

head flat with the ball end of a chasing hammer until the rivet is flush with the back of the metal.

Rivets may also be used as a means of attaching beads or pearls to metal. Solder lengths of wire slightly longer than the bead diameter to the metal surface, thread the bead over the wire then make two saw cuts at right angles to each other on the projecting end of the wire. This forms a bifurcated type rivet which can be opened out sufficiently to retain the bead in position.

Figure 97   Side section showing the rivet through the bead
Figure 98   Plan view showing the rivet opened out

SOFT SOLDERING This is the easiest of the two methods of soldering and can be used with brass or copper but must not be used for soldering silver. It is preferable to use an electric soldering iron for soldering small components together. The soldering iron must be kept well tinned in order to retain solder on the tip of the iron. To do this, heat the soldering iron to normal working temperature and then clean the tip with an old file or piece of emery cloth. Paint the cleaned area quickly with flux and coat the tip of the hot soldering iron by touching a strip of solder. Best quality tinsmith's solder is recommended.

The areas to be joined together must be thoroughly cleaned and carefully fluxed with any of the commercial liquid fluxes available for soft soldering. Joints must fit together well and be kept in contact whilst touching with the soldering iron. Simple clips made of wire, bent nails or split pins can all be used for holding components together for soldering.

HARD SOLDERING This process requires more skill to master than soft soldering but because it is much more versatile for complicated assemblies and gives a much stronger joint, it is recommended that this method is used wherever possible. It is, of course, essential for soldering silver articles.

There are three grades of hard or silver solders available called *Hard, Medium* and *Easy*. Each grade of solder has a different melting point which enables assemblies that require successive solderings to be accomplished. The solder with the highest melting point which is Hard solder is used for the first assembly, Medium for the second and finally Easy solder which has the lowest melting point of the three. Do not confuse the term *Easy solder* with *soft solder*.

It is essential that the joint areas to be soldered should be free of dirt and should fit closely together. Use soft iron binding wire or clips to secure the parts together ready for soldering. Paint the joint area with a flux of borax and water mixed to a creamy consistency using a soft paint brush.

The two main methods of applying solder to a joint are strip soldering using a strip of solder held with pliers and letting it melt and flow along the joint and soldering with tiny pieces of solder known as *pallions* which are laid along a joint. The solder itself must be clean and painted with flux. The paint brush, dipped in wet borax, can be used to place the pallions along the fluxed joint but it must never be used when the metal is hot as it will stick to the metal and burn. Tweezers should be used when the metal is hot either to replace pallions that have moved out of place or to add more solder to the joint.

The article to be soldered should be placed on a hearth or asbestos block and the flame from the jeweler's blowpipe or blowtorch gently played upon it. Care should be taken to heat the whole article gradually first before concentrating the heat on the joint area. When the joint area is at the correct temperature (red-hot) the solder will melt and join the pieces together. Solder always runs to the hottest part, therefore it is essential to heat the joint area evenly. Remove clips or binding wire before pickling and then place the assembled piece of work in the safety pickle until the flux has been dissolved and oxides removed.

If the design requires a number of small components to be soldered together at the same time, it may be necessary to place them in plaster to keep each component in the required position while soldering. First, place the component on plasticine in the required position for assembly and build a shallow wall of plasticine round the perimeter of the piece of work, then pour a slurry of plaster of paris within the walled area to a depth of approximately 4·5 mm ($\frac{3}{16}$ in.).

Allow the plaster to dry out thoroughly and then remove the plasticine. The piece of work, now partly embedded in plaster, should be carefully brushed with petrol (gasoline) to remove all unwanted traces of plasticine. Apply the flux to all the joint areas and solder with *pallions* placed along the edges to be joined, heating the piece of work very gently at first to allow the petrol to burn off. After soldering, quench the piece of work in cold water to disintegrate the plaster, and then pickle.

Methods of Assembly

There are several methods of assembly which could be used. The methods vary considerably in their requirements, both in degrees of skill and equipment. Hard soldering using silver and gold solders gives the best results but is the most skilful and expensive form of assembly. Any jewelry made of silver must be soldered with silver solder and must comply with the standards specified by the Assay Office (the Bureau of Commercial Standards in the US). If hard soldering proves to be too expensive and difficult, soft soldering using lead solder is quite suitable for working with copper and brass. As well as soldering, pieces of metal can be joined together by linking or riveting. These two methods impose certain conditions on designs and the assembly method should therefore be considered at the design stage. An adhesive such as *Araldite* epoxy can be used to glue pearls, beads or imitation stones to settings and could also be used to glue small pieces of metal together. This method will not have the permanency of other methods but could be used with younger children. *Perspex* can be linked, riveted or glued together with perspex cement. Wood can be linked or joined together with adhesive.

LINKING   drilling holes, annealing and pickling, making links.

This is one of the simplest and most effective methods of assembly. Links are made of either wire or metal strip and they can vary in size and shape. Holes are drilled in the units to be joined together and the links are threaded through and then closed with pliers. When working with silver it is advisable to solder the links together for added strength and to prevent any loss caused by links coming apart.

Drilling holes It is advisable to use a centre punch to make a location point before drilling a hole. This prevents the drill moving from the desired position and scratching the surface of the metal. Always centre punch sheet metal against a flat metal surface otherwise the sheet will become blemished on the underside. To hold the metal rigid and flat for drilling by hand, clamp the unit in a vice against a wooden block (*figure 91*).

Casting Methods

Casting with cuttlefish bone Cuttlefish bone is a very suitable material for making simple moulds where only one casting is required. This material can be obtained from jeweler's suppliers and sometimes from pet shops. It is preferable to obtain as large a bone as possible so that it can be cut in half to form the two sides of the mould. Two smaller, separate bones can be used if they are rubbed smooth and flat on one side with emery paper wrapped round a block of wood, and if the top of the two bones is cut off to allow sufficient width of bone for the funnel.

Figure 99

Figure 100

Create the design in one half of the cuttlefish bone, either by working from a model of a preconceived idea, or by working directly into the bone with various tools, always remembering that you are working in reverse. Cut an adequate funnel shape at the top of the mould and scratch several air vents from the design to near the funnel area so that trapped air can escape when the molten metal is poured in (*figure 100*).

Figure 101

The two halves should be firmly bound together with soft iron binding wire and maintained in an upright position supported by fire clay bricks (*figure 101*). Pewter can be melted in a plumber's ladle over a gas ring. Aluminium can be melted in a refractory clay crucible with a blow torch. The molten metal should then be poured continuously either from the ladle or crucible into the mould until the funnel is full. It is recommended that this is done in an area protected with asbestos sheeting, in case of any spillage.

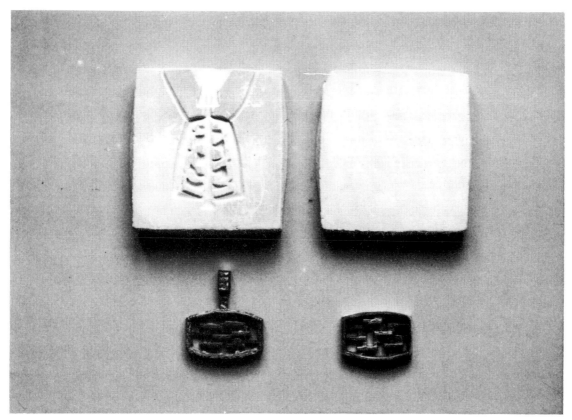

Alternative moulds can be made by casting blocks of dental
or investment casting materials (*figure 102*). It is advisable
to follow the supplier's instructions for mixing these
materials.

Figure 102

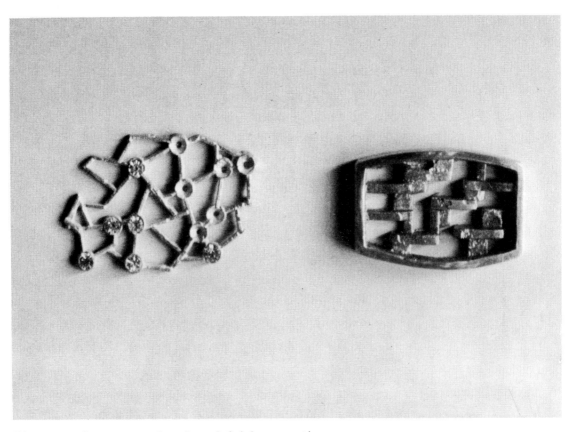

Figure 103 shows examples of cuttlefish bone castings.

The Solbrig casting process   This is a method of casting in which steam pressure forces molten metal into a mould. Silver is the best metal to use for this.

Models must first be prepared in dental wax or beeswax and then set on a wax cone base (*figure 104*). Use thin dental wax wire for sprues or runners to connect the models to the cone.

The wax cone must be firmly attached to a sheet of glass or flat sheet of base metal and both must be coated with a parting agent such as *Vaseline*. A copper tube or preferably a stainless steel flask, obtainable from investment casting suppliers, is then placed around the wax structure (*figure 105*). The outer edge of the flask adjoining the base plate must be sealed with plasticine to prevent any leakage when the wet investment material is poured into the flask. Mix the investment material according to the supplier's instructions and then pour gently down the side of the flask until it is full, taking care not to damage the wax models inside. Some air bubbles may remain trapped inside the flask; it is possible to remove some of them by gently tapping the base plate to vibrate the investment material.

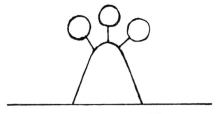

Figure 104

Leave the investment for several hours to set completely, then remove the plasticine seal and separate the flask from the base plate. It is advisable to place the flask in a warm area to allow the investment material to dry out completely. To burn out the wax from the flask, heat slowly with the blowtorch until red-hot. This completes the process for preparing a mould ready to receive the molten metal.

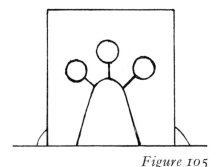

Figure 105

The mould should now be inverted so that the space left by the wax cone becomes the well or reservoir in which small pieces of silver will be melted. Make sure that the reservoir contains sufficient silver to fill the mould. To obtain the steam pressure, dampen the asbestos pad attached to the press arm before proceeding with the melt. Heat the silver with a blowtorch until the metal reaches a fluid state and then clamp the dampened pad on top of the mould (*figures 106 and 107*). This method of casting will produce very good results from simple and inexpensive equipment but it does require some experience to master the technique. It is possible to either make or obtain this equipment.

Centrifugal casting is another process of casting which gives superior results but as it requires considerable financial outlay to purchase this equipment the process is outside the scope of this book.

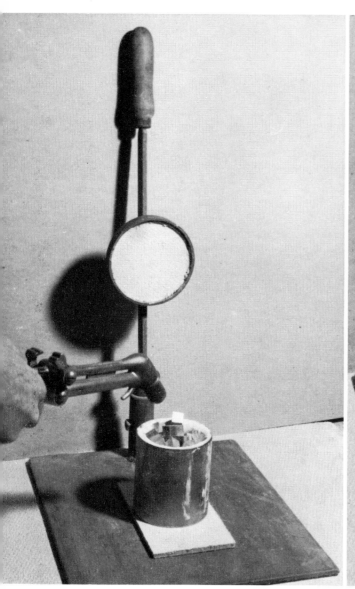

Figure 106

Figure 107

Finishing Processes

Metal finishing is done in two stages, first by hand and then by machine. It is necessary to remove all scratches and blemishes by carefully rubbing the surface of the metal with abrasives such as emery cloth, pumice stone and Water of Ayr stone. Coarser abrasives should be used first, followed by progressively finer abrasives until all unwanted defects are removed. It is advisable to change the direction of rubbing or grinding with each grade of abrasive used. Pumice stone and Water of Ayr stone both have to be applied with plenty of water.

After all the defects have been removed by hand the piece of work can then be polished by means of various mops attached to a polishing motor spindle. Primary polishing should be done using *Tripoli* compound on canvas mops or bristle brushes for polishing chain or textured areas. Never polish chain holding the length in the hand and never hold a piece of work in a cloth while polishing because both chains and cloths are liable to become entangled round the spindle of the polishing machine and serious accidents could be the result of this action. Chain should be held against a rigid surface such as a block of wood.

Use rouge composition on a soft calico (cotton) mop followed by a silver polish on a lambswool mop for final polishing. The piece of work should be cleaned between each successive stage of polishing to remove surplus polishing compounds and to prevent the polishing mops from becoming clogged up with a mixture of polishing compounds. Use methylated spirit (alcohol) to dissolve the polishing compounds and then wash in warm soapy water. Never use different polishing compounds on the same mop. Mops can be cleaned by holding a stiff wire brush against them while they are revolving on the polishing machine. Certain awkward areas where machine polishing is impractical may require string polishing or hand burnishing to obtain a finish.

Figure 108

It is possible to obtain a colour contrast for parts of a piece of jewelry by oxidization. This process is suitable for silver, copper and pewter. The piece of work may either be totally immersed in a solution of ammonium sulphide or certain areas can be painted with the solution. Various tones are possible depending on the strength and temperature of the solution. A strong hot solution will give a very dark grey colour. High relief areas can be polished by hand with a soft cloth impregnated with a silver polish.

To finish *Perspex*, first use garnet papers to remove saw and file marks. Garnet paper is recommended because it is less susceptible to clogging. *Perspex* can then be lightly polished with rouge composition on a soft calico mop, followed by a silver polish on a lambswool mop. Do not press the piece of work too hard against the mop as the friction could overheat the *Perspex* and melt it. Do not use a spirit (alcohol) solvent on *Perspex* as this will dissolve it, merely wash in warm soapy water.

Wooden jewelry can be completely finished and polished by hand. First use grades of emery paper or garnet paper to completely remove all scratch and file marks and then polish with furniture wax polish or cream to emphasize the grain.

Further Reading

Metalwork and Enamelling, Herbert Maryon, Chapman and Hall London

Metal Techniques for Craftsmen, Oppi Untracht, Robert Hale London

Metalwork Designs of Today, Brian Larkman, John Murray London

Introducing Jewelry Making, John Crawford, Batsford London, Watson-Guptill New York

Introducing Enamelling, Valerie Conway, Batsford London, Watson-Guptill New York

The Technique of Enamelling, Geoffrey Clarke, Francis and Ida Feher, Batsford London, Van Nostrand Reinhold New York

Creative Metal Craft, Heinz Ullrich and Dieter Klante, Batsford London, Van Nostrand Reinhold New York

Collecting and Polishing Stones, Herbert Scarfe, Batsford London

Cutting and Setting Stones, Herbert Scarfe, Batsford London, Watson-Guptill New York

Suppliers UK

Base metals
H. J. Edwards and Sons (B'ham)
Limited
93–95 Barr Street
Birmingham 19

Precious metals
Johnson Matthey Metals Limited
73–78 Hatton Garden
London EC1P 1DB and
Victoria Street
Birmingham
also supply silver solder and findings

Tools
Charles Cooper (Hatton Garden)
Limited
12 Hatton Wall
Hatton Garden
London EC1
also suppliers of polishing materials
and findings

E. Gray and Son
12 Clerkenwell Road
London EC1

Herring, Morgan and Southon Limited
9 Berwick Street
London W1
also supply jewelry findings

George Panton and Sons
Buchanan Street
Glasgow

T. Sutton
166 Warstone Lane
Birmingham 18

Casting materials
W. J. Hooker Limited
Waterside
Brightlingsea
Colchester
Essex
also supply flasks

Hoben Davis Limited
Holditch Industrial Estate
Spencroft Road
Newcastle-under-Lyme
Staffordshire
also suppliers of safety pickle and
golden carving wax

General craft materials
Art and Crafts Unlimited
49 Shelton Street
London WC2

Dryad
Northgates
Leicester
also suppliers of *Perspex* off-cuts and
wooden beads

Suppliers USA

Gold, silver, copper, tools, enamels, findings, general craft materials
Allcraft
22 West 48th Street
New York, New York 10036

American Handicraft Company Inc
20 West 14th Street
New York, New York 10011

Anchor Tool and Supply Company Inc
12 John Street
New York, New York 10038

DRS
110 West 47th Street
New York, New York 10036

Findings
Krieger and Dranoff
44 West 47th Street
New York, New York 10036

Hagstoz and Son
709 Sansom Street
Philadelphia, Pennsylvania 19106

Sculpture materials
Sculpture Associates Limited
114 East 25th Street
New York, New York 10010

Sculpture House
38 East 30th Street
New York, New York 10016

Sculpture Service Inc
9 East 19th Street
New York, New York 10003

Art supplies, tools, plaster
A. I. Freidman Inc
25 West 45th Street
New York, New York 10036

Arthur Brown and Brothers Inc
2 West 46th Street
New York, New York 10036

Polyester resins
Resin Coatings Corporation
14950 N.W. Court
Opa Locka, Florida 33054

Polyproducts Corporation
Order Department, Room 25
13810 Nelson Avenue
Detroit, Michigan 48227

Stones
Nathan Gem and Pearl Company Inc
18 East 48th Street
New York, New York 10017

International Gem
15 Maiden Lane
New York, New York 10038

Figure 109   Coral   ▶

Index

Adhesives 9, 11, 15, 62, 78–9
Aluminium 55, 56, 82
Annealing 72
Asbestos 61
Assembly of parts 70–9

Bakers fluid 61
Balsa wood 9, 11, 30
Bangles 23 *see also* Bracelets
Beads 62
Beeswax 9, 45, 85
Belts 15
Bench 58
    bench peg 58, 66
Blowpipe, French (for soldering) 60, 77
Board, for laying out models 9
Borax (for soldering) 60, 77
Bracelets 12, 15, 34 *see also* Bangles
Brass 55, 56, 76
Brooches 20, 22, 34

Cardboard 9, 11, 14, 32
    tubes 9, 23, 24
    models 16
    bending 32
Casting 44–5, 55, 56, 57
    centrifugal 85
    using cuttlefish bone 79–82
    Solbrig process 84–5
Centrifugal casting 85
Chain 42–3
    polishing 85
Cleaning 70–1, 87 *see also* Finishing

processes; Pickling; Polishing
Copper 55–6, 76
Cutting 64–9
Cuttlefish bone 44, 61, 79–82

Dental (Investment) casting materials 62, 83, 84
Design
    ideas for 7, 10, 13, 14, 15, 16, 20, 24, 26, 29, 30
    principles of 7–8 *see also* Model making
    see also individual articles,
        eg Bracelets; Sculptured jewelry; Texture
Dividers, spring 59
Dowelling 9, 16, 28
Drill
    electric for polishing 58
    attachments 61
    hand 58
Drilling 79

Ear-rings 13, 34
Emery paper 61
Enamelling 12

Files 60, 70
Finishing processes 87–89
Fire-clay bricks 62

Gas ring 58

Hammered effects 35–9
Hammers 35, 38, 59

Investment (dental) casting material 62, 83, 84

Jewelry making techniques *see* Annealing; Assembly of parts; Casting; Cutting; Finishing processes; Model making; Riveting; Soldering Jewels
  semi-precious and synthetic 44

Knife 9

Linked designs 12, 13, 74
  joining links 79

Macaroni 9, 28
Mallet 59
Mallotte (French blowpipe) 60, 77
Mandrel (Triblet) 32, 60
Materials
  modelmaking 9
  jewelry making 55, 61–2
Melting points of metals 56–7
Metals
  bar
  bending 16, 30, 32
  casting 44–5, 55, 56, 57, 79–85
  pre-formed objects and sections 50–53, 62
  sheet 10, 15
    cutting 64–9
  strip 16
  texturing 35–41
Metals 55–7
  Aluminium 55, 56, 82
  Brass 55, 56, 76
  Copper 55–6, 76
  Pewter 55, 56
  Silver 55, 57, 76, 79
  Melting points 56, 57
Model making 8

materials 9
  for cast jewelry 44–5
  for sculptured jewelry 46
Nails 62
Necklaces 13, 34
Oxidation 12, 88
Paint
  metallic spray 9, 11, 22, 30
Paint brush 60
Paper 9
Pencil 9
Pendants 13, 20, 22, 34
Perspec 10, 79
  cutting 69
  polishing 88
  riveting 75
Pewter 55, 56
Pickle, safety (for de-oxidation) 61, 73
Pins and thread 9
Plaster of paris 9, 46, 62 77–8
Plasticine 9, 46, 78
Pliers 59, 70
Plumbers cradle 56, 60
Polish 61
Polishing 87, 89
  attachments 61, 87
Punch, centre 58, 79
Pyrex glass dish 60

Rings 19, 32
  ring sizes 60
Riveting 11, 75–6, 78
Rods 28
  cutting 69
Rouge composition 61, 87
Ruler 9, 59
Saw
  coping 58, 69

Saw *continued*
    eclipse 58, 69
    piercing 28, 58, 64–8
    tenon 58
Scissors 9
Scriber 59
Sculptured jewelry 44–8
    metal cast 44–5
    wood 46–8
Shears 58, 69
Sheet materials 10–19
    cutting 64–9
    linked designs 12–13
    random line patterns 14–15
    unit designs 12
    and wire 64–9
Silver 55, 57, 76, 79
Silver solder *see* Soldering, hard
Solbrig casting process 84–5
Soldering 11, 61
    hard 76–8
    soft 76
Soldering iron, electric 58, 76
Spaghetti 9, 22
Sparex (safety pickle) 61, 73
Stones
    semi-precious and artificial 44
Sulphuric acid 73

Techniques *see* Annealing; Assembly of parts; Castings; Cutting; Finishing processes; Model making; Riveting; Soldering
Texture 35–41
    using hammers 35–8
    using nails 39–41
Tools
    jewelry making 58–60
    model making 8, 9
Triblet 32, 60
Tubes 28 *see also under* Cardboard
Tweezers 58

Vice
    engineers 58
    hand 59, 70
    pin 59, 70

Wax (for cast models) 44–5
Wire 19, 22, 24
    iron binding wire 61
    Random line patterns 20
    and sheet materials 22
Wood
    balsa 9, 11, 30
    burning 48
    dowelling 9, 16, 28
    finishing and polishing 89
    qualities of 46
    sculptured designs 46–8